Digital Marketing 2023

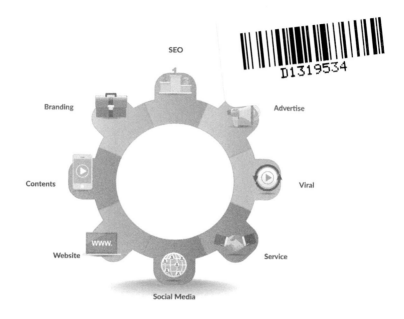

The Ultimate Guide to dominating your competition and winning as a Digital Marketer in 2023

Brandon W Raybon Sr.

1

Printed in the United States of America
First Printing, 2022

ISBN 9798360497677

Preface

Hi, my name is Brandon, and I am a content marketer. I worked as a Marketing Director for six years for the Alabama Army National Guard and am presently retired from Active Duty. During that time, I worked alongside some of the brightest minds in the country. Trained with Apple, Google, and other fortune 500 companies and learned the full spectrum of Marketing and advertising.

I am currently a freelance content marketer. I am responsible for researching industry-related topics, preparing well-structured drafts, and using digital publishing platforms. Some other incredible things I do daily are creating and distributing marketing copy to promote our company and products, interviewing industry professionals, and incorporating their views in blog posts.

I conduct keyword research daily while using search engine optimization for content, promote it on social networks, and monitor engagement.

I am confident in my skills as a writer and storyteller. I firmly understand the latest trends in digital marketing and social media. And I am passionate about helping businesses grow through effective content marketing strategies.

As we move into 2023, the door is wide open for businesses to surpass what was expected five years ago. We have technology that has far surpassed anything I can imagine. With marketing tools like marketing automation, CRMs, Inbound marketing, and AI becoming more mainstream, it is now easier to connect and convert our audience into customers.

As a marketing professional, I have always prided myself on being an expert in my field. But when I made a big mistake in marketing that almost cost me my career, I realized how much I still had to learn about this ever-changing industry.

It all started one afternoon when I received a frantic call from our clients. Our marketing campaign had been a total failure, and the client was agitated. I tried to defend my actions by saying this was just a temporary setback, but deep down, I knew I had made a colossal mistake.

Over the next few weeks, I spent countless hours researching and trying to understand what went wrong. I learned that marketing is constantly evolving and that I needed to stay up-to-date with the latest trends and best practices to succeed.

Thankfully, my mistake became a valuable learning experience, and I emerged from it more knowledgeable and determined than ever before. If someone had told me about the importance of marketing research and staying on top of industry changes, I probably wouldn't have made that big mistake in the first place. But now that I know better, I am committed to never making that same mistake again.

This led me to create this short book to help others in the Marketing and Advertising field not make the same mistakes I did. I hope you find this book's insights and wisdom useful, and I wish you all the best on your marketing journey.

Intro

Online marketing is constantly evolving and changing. What worked in 2022 may not work in 2023. This book will explore the online marketing trends expected to dominate in 2023. We will also look at how these trends may differ from 2022. By understanding the coming changes, you can be prepared to adapt and stay ahead of your competition.

As I sit down to write this, I can't help but feel a sense of dread. Every day, the landscape of online marketing is changing. And as someone who's trying to stay ahead of the curve, it can be hard to keep up.

I remember when video marketing was starting to take off. I was so excited about it – sure, it would take a little bit more work, but the potential payoff was there. So I started creating videos for my business… and they tanked. I had no idea what I was doing wrong.

It was only later that I learned about things like SEO and metadata. If I had known back then what I know now, my videos might have done a lot better.

Social media has been another tricky area. Every platform is different, and you need to be on all of them to succeed. But trying to keep up with all of them is practically impossible.

And then there's mobile marketing. With more and more people using their phones to browse the internet, it's become more important than ever to make your site mobile-friendly. But that's only sometimes easy or cheap to do.

All of this makes me wish I could return and start my business over again. But then I remembered that even if I did, the landscape of online marketing would still be changing by the time I got there. So instead, I'll have to keep learning and trying my best to stay ahead of the curve.

CHAPTER ONE

The changing landscape of online marketing

When I started my business, I was eager to learn all I could learn about online marketing. I read article after article, trying to absorb as much information as possible.

At the time, I mainly focused on search engine optimization and paid advertising. I knew those were two of the most important aspects of online marketing, so I focused on them.

But as time passed, I realized I needed to keep up with the latest trends. That meant paying attention to changes in search engine algorithms, social media platforms, and other aspects of online marketing.

To keep up with the constantly evolving world of online marketing, staying current on the latest trends is essential. That means being aware of changes in search engine algorithms, social media platforms, and other aspects of online marketing.

It can be challenging to keep track of all the changes, but doing your best is essential. By understanding the latest trends, you can give your business the best chance for success.

Some of the latest trends in online marketing include using video content, focusing on mobile users, and using influencers to market your products or services. These are just a few examples, so stay up to date on all the latest trends.

The landscape of online marketing is constantly changing, so it's crucial to stay ahead of the curve. By staying up to date on the latest trends, you can give your business the best chance for success.

The internet is constantly evolving

The internet is an ever-changing landscape. In the early days of the internet, it was primarily used for communication purposes, such as email and chat rooms. However, in recent years the internet has evolved into a global marketplace. Now, businesses can reach consumers worldwide with a simple online presence. Additionally, social media has given people a platform to share their thoughts and ideas with others. As the internet continues to evolve, it is becoming increasingly crucial for businesses to have a solid online presence.

According to a study by Clutch, "*97 percent of businesses that have a website believe that it is important to their success.*" Furthermore, 79 percent of businesses say their website is the most effective way to reach new customers. Having a website is essential for any business looking to grow.

Another aspect of the internet that is constantly evolving is social media. Social media has recently become an important tool for marketing and customer engagement. For example, Facebook now has over 2 billion active users. This provides businesses with a huge potential audience for their products and services. Additionally, social media platforms allow businesses to connect with customers more personally than traditional advertising methods.

The internet is constantly evolving, and businesses that keep up will be kept up. The best way to stay ahead of the curve is to have a robust online presence and use social media to do this. By doing so, businesses can reach more people and grow their business exponentially.

What worked yesterday might not work today

Online marketing is constantly evolving, and what worked yesterday might not work today. For example, in the early days of online marketing, spam was a highly effective way to promote a business or product. However, as consumers became savvier about identifying and avoiding spam, companies had to find new and more creative ways to market their products online.

Another example is search engine optimization (SEO). In the early days of SEO, compa could get away with using black hat techniques like keyword stuffing and link schemes to boost their search engine rankings. However, as Google began to crack down on these techniques, businesses had to adopt more sophisticated and sustainable SEO strategies.

So what does this mean for businesses looking to market their products online? It means that they must constantly innovate and evolve their marketing strategies to keep up with the latest trends. They also need to be willing to experiment with new tactics and technologies to see what works best for them.

Marketers need to be agile and adapt to change

Marketing today is a constantly evolving field. The internet has completely changed how marketing works, and it's now more important than ever for marketers to be agile and adapt to change.

One of the most important aspects of online marketing is staying up to date with the latest trends and changes in technology. If you're not keeping up with the latest trends, your competitors will be, and they will leave you behind. Blogging is still a thing. According to Hubspot, "*48% of companies that have a content marketing strategy leverage blogging.*" *(HubSpot Blog Research, 2021) (Source: https://www.hubspot.com/marketing-statistics)*

Another important aspect of online marketing is using the latest tools and platforms. If you're not using the latest tools, you're not reaching your target audience in the most effective way possible.

Finally, online marketing requires a lot of flexibility. The internet is constantly changing, so you need to be able to change with it. If your marketing strategy needs to be fixed, you need to be able to adapt and try something new.

Changes in the online marketing landscape

In the last decade, there have been some significant changes in the online marketing landscape. The most notable of these changes has been the massive growth of social media platforms like Facebook and Twitter. These platforms have given businesses a new way to reach out to potential customers, and they've proven incredibly effective.

Another significant change has been the growth of search engine optimization (SEO). SEO is the process of optimizing a website so that it can rank higher in search engine results pages (SERPs). This has become increasingly important over the years as more people use search engines to find information online.

Finally, there has been a shift toward video content in recent years. Videos are a very effective way of engaging potential customers, and they're also great for SEO. As a result, more and more businesses are starting to invest in video marketing campaigns.

All of these changes have significantly impacted the online marketing landscape, and they're likely to continue to do so in the years ahead. Businesses need to stay up-to-date with these changes if they want to be successful in the online space.

CHAPTER TWO

The rise of video marketing

Video is one of the most popular forms of content

I remember the first time I used video as a marketing tool. I was a small business owner, and I was trying to find ways to market my business online. I had heard about video marketing, but I needed to figure out how it would work for me.

I decided to give it a try, and I created a short video about my business. I uploaded it to YouTube and shared it on my Facebook page. I was surprised by how well the video did. It got a lot of views, and it helped me to connect with my customers.

Since then, I've continued using video as a marketing tool, which has been a massive success for my business. Video is an effective way to communicate your message and can help you build trust with your customers.

Video marketing is on the rise. With social media platforms like Facebook and Instagram making it easier for businesses to share videos with their followers, more and more companies are beginning to see the value in using video as a marketing tool. We must diversify our marketing efforts as one area will not work. This from WARC, *"YouTube's fortunes have also proven vulnerable to privacy changes on Apple devices; WARC believes that YouTube's advertising revenue will rise 7.3% this year (compared to +45.9% in 2021), but that its growth will then ease to 5.6% in 2023."* This means that a Youtube channel alone will not help your clients with growth.

Video can be a very effective way to market your business. Not only is it engaging and eye-catching, but it can also be a very effective way to communicate your message. Video can help you to build trust with your customers, and it can also help you to create a connection with them.

In addition to using video for marketing purposes, you can also use it for branding purposes. For example, a well-made video can help to promote your brand and allow people to learn more about what your brand represents.

If you're looking to start using video as a marketing tool, there are a few things that you should keep in mind:

First, ensure that your videos are high quality and accurately reflect your brand.

When creating videos for your business, it is essential to ensure they are high quality and accurately reflect your brand. In addition, your videos should be professionally produced, edited, and aligned with your overall branding strategy.

Your videos should also be relevant to your target audience. Make sure that you are creating videos relevant to your customers and addressing the needs and concerns of your target market.

Finally, ensure you use the proper marketing channels to distribute your videos. For example, platforms like Facebook and Instagram are great for sharing videos. Still, you may consider using other platforms, such as YouTube or Vimeo, to reach a wider audience.

Second, ensure that your videos are appropriately targeted - ensure they are reaching the right people and providing them with valuable information.

When creating videos for your business, you must ensure they are correctly targeted. This means making sure that they are reaching the right people and providing them with valuable information.

To target your videos properly, you'll need to know your audience. You'll need to understand their needs and what information they are looking for. Once you know this, you can create tailored videos to meet these needs.

Your videos should also be relevant to your audience. They should be addressing the issues that are important to them and providing them with solutions. Viewers who feel like you understand them and their needs will be more likely to trust you and consider your products or services.

And finally, make sure that you're promoting your videos effectively - post them on social media, embed them on your website, and share them with your followers.

One of the best ways to promote your videos is to post them on social media. Make sure to post them on your Facebook page, your Twitter account, and your Instagram account. You can also embed them on your website and share them with your followers.

Posting your videos on social media is a great way to reach a larger audience, and it's also a great way to engage with your customers. And embedding your videos on your website is a great way to keep your customers engaged with your business.

Get user-generated content and use it in your marketing plan. According to MARCOM, *"Brands don't have to overextend themselves and produce all their marketing collateral and content on their own. A great way to lighten the workload on marketing teams while highlighting customers is to leverage user-generated content (UGC). UGC is more authentic and trustworthy because it comes from a brand's customers and advocates. In fact,90% of users trust UGC to inform their purchasing decisions."* You must tap into your customers.

Sharing your videos with your followers is a great way to let them know what you're up to, and it's also a great way to keep them connected with your business. So make sure to post, embed, and share your videos!

People are more likely to watch a video than read an article

People are more likely to watch a video than read an article. According to a study done by Nielsen, *"online video now accounts for 50 percent of all mobile traffic and 64 percent of all traffic on home networks."* That's lots of people watching videos! Not only that, but the average person watches over an hour and a half of online video content each day. It all adds up to many people spending time watching videos instead of reading articles.

So why are people so drawn to video content? There are a few reasons. For one, videos are more engaging than articles. People are more likely to stay interested in a video than an article, which means they're more likely to watch the whole thing. Videos also allow you to see and hear the information in action, which can help understand complicated topics. Finally, videos are great for sharing information quickly and easily. For example, a video is the best way to do it if you want to share a news story or explain a concept.

Videos can be used for various purposes, such as product demonstrations, educational content, or brand awareness

Video content has become one of the most popular means of communication in recent years. Its versatility has made it a valuable tool for various purposes, including product demonstrations, educational content, and brand awareness.

Product demonstrations are one of the most common uses for video content. By showcasing a product in action, companies can show potential customers what it can do and how it works. This can be especially helpful for products that are difficult to demonstrate through text or images alone. Educational content is another widespread use for videos. By providing clear, concise explanations of complex topics, videos can help students learn more effectively. And finally, brand awareness is an important goal for many businesses. In addition, videos can create engaging content that attracts attention and promotes the company's products or services.

All of these uses demonstrate the versatility of video content and its ability to reach a broad audience. Videos can be an extremely effective way to communicate with consumers and promote a business's products or services.

CHAPTER THREE

Social media and its impact on marketing

Social media is a powerful tool that can be used for marketing

We must understand that social media will continue to dominate marketing in 2023, but some trends are dropping with changes in the technology space. According to WARC, *"the impact of Apple's privacy measures on social media companies that rely on cross-site tracking will be in the region of a $40bn hit to their bottom lines over the course of this and the coming year. Most are expected to see far less growth than they are used to over the forecast period. Overall, social is expected to rise 11.5% (compared to +47.1% in 2021) in 2023 before cooling to just 5.2% - its slowest-ever period of growth."* Social media will still be a large chunk of your advertising budget for 2023, even with the growth slowing down to 5.2%.

When it comes to marketing, social media can be a potent tool. I know this from personal experience, as I've successfully used social media to market my own business.

I started my business a few years ago, and at the time, I was still determining how to go about marketing it. I knew I needed to do something, but I needed to figure out what that was. So, I turned to social media.

I began by creating a Facebook page for my business and posting regularly. I also made a Twitter account and started tweeting about my business. And finally, I set up a blog and started writing blog posts about my business.

The results were terrific. Within a few months, my business had grown significantly. I attribute this growth mainly to my effective use of social media for marketing purposes.

So, social media is the way to go if you're looking for a way to market your business effectively. It's a powerful tool that can help you reach many people quickly and easily.

It can help to reach a wider audience, build brand awareness, and generate leads

Online marketing and social media are powerful tools that can be used to reach a wider audience, build brand awareness, and generate leads. By creating compelling content and using effective marketing techniques, businesses can connect with more potential customers and increase their sales.

Social media is a particularly effective tool for reaching a wider audience. By creating profiles on social networks and using targeted advertising, businesses can connect with more people who may be interested in their products or services. Additionally, social media provides a platform for engaging with customers and building relationships. This can help to create brand loyalty and encourage customers to return to your business in the future.

Generating leads is another important benefit of online marketing and social media. By using lead capture forms, businesses can collect information about potential customers who may be interested in their products or services. This information can then be used to contact these potential customers or send targeted advertisements. Remember, online marketing and social media allow businesses to find a wider audience, expand brand awareness, and generate leads.

However, it is vital to use social media wisely, as it can also have adverse effects

When used correctly, social media can be a solid marketing tool for your business. However, it is important to be aware of the potential negative effects of social media use. For example, mishandling your social media accounts can lead to negative publicity for your business, loss of customers, and even lawsuits.

It is important to use social media wisely to avoid these negative consequences. Here are some tips for using social media effectively in your business:

1. *Make sure all your social media accounts are accurate and up-to-date.*

First impressions are everything, especially when it comes to businesses. As more and more people turn to social media for information about products and services, businesses must ensure their accounts are accurate and up-to-date. A few simple steps can make a big difference. For example, regularly check to ensure that your profile photos and cover images are current. Then, respond to comments and messages in a timely fashion. And take the time to fully fill out your profile description, using keywords that potential customers are likely to search for. Taking these steps can help ensure that your business makes a great first impression on social media.

2. *Be sure to post relevant and informative content that will interest your customers.*

Maintaining an active social media presence is essential for any business looking to connect with its customers. However, simply having a profile on Facebook or Twitter is not enough - businesses need to make sure they are posting relevant and informative content that will interest their customers. This means staying up-to-date on industry news and developments and sharing timely and relevant information with your followers. It also means keeping your tone light and engaging so that customers will want to keep coming back for more. By taking the time to post interesting and informative content, you can build a strong relationship with your customers - and turn them into lifelong fans.

3.   *Monitor your social media accounts regularly and respond promptly to comments or inquiries.*

Maintaining an active presence on social media is essential for any business. Not only does it help you connect with potential and existing customers, it also allows you to stay up-to-date with what people say about your brand. That's why it's essential to regularly monitor your business social media accounts and respond promptly to any comments or inquiries. By doing so, you can resolve any issues quickly and effectively and build stronger relationships with your customers in the process. So don't let your social media presence fall by the wayside - make sure to stay on top of it, and you'll reap the rewards.

4.   *Avoid posting negative or inflammatory comments about your competitors or other businesses.*

In the business world, it's crucial to maintain a positive attitude and avoid posting negative or inflammatory comments about your competitors or other businesses. Not only does this reflect poorly on your company, but it can also damage your relationships with other businesses. Furthermore, it can give your competitors an edge by allowing them to focus on their strengths while you're busy dealing with negative feedback.

Of course, there will be times when you're unhappy with a competitor's product or service. However, it's essential to handle these situations professionally. You can express your dissatisfaction publicly but avoid name-calling or making personal attacks. Instead, focus on constructive criticism that will improve the situation for everyone involved. By taking the high road, you'll foster a positive business environment and build strong relationships with other businesses.

5.   *Be aware of the potential legal implications of social media use in your industry.*

Social media has become an integral part of many people's lives in today's connected world. However, few people stop to think about the potential legal implications of their social media use. Depending on your industry, strict regulations may govern what you can and cannot say online. For example, in the healthcare industry, HIPAA compliance is essential for protecting patient privacy. Meanwhile, in the financial sector, insider trading laws prevent employees from sharing certain information about their company. Violating these laws can lead to hefty fines or even jail time. As such, knowing the potential legal implications of social media use in your industry is important. You can avoid legal trouble down the road by taking a few simple precautions.

By following these tips, you can use social media safely and effectively to promote your business.

CHAPTER FOUR

Mobile marketing and its growth

Mobile devices are the main source for access the internet

Mobile devices have become the only source for accessing the internet. This is evident in the growth of mobile marketing. As more people use their mobile devices to go online, businesses are taking notice and starting to create campaigns specifically for mobile users.

There are many reasons for the growth of mobile marketing. One reason is that people use their mobile devices more often than ever. In addition, mobile devices allow users to access the internet anywhere they go. This makes them a powerful tool for marketing purposes.

Another factor contributing to mobile marketing growth is the increasing number of available mobile devices. Smartphones and tablets are becoming more common, helping drive up mobile content and applications demand.

Overall, it is clear that mobile marketing is growing rapidly. However, businesses that want to reach a wider audience should consider creating optimized campaigns for mobile devices.

This means that more and more people are using their phones to consume content

As the use of mobile devices continues to grow, businesses are taking note and adapting their marketing strategies to reach this growing audience. Mobile marketing involves creating content and advertising specifically designed for consumption on mobile devices. This can include anything from text messages to videos to apps.

One reason mobile marketing is becoming increasingly popular is that more and more people are using their phones to consume content. In fact, according to a report by ComScore, in 2017, *"78% of all U.S. adults accessed the internet via a mobile device."* Therefore, your business must have a strong mobile marketing strategy to reach the largest possible audience.

Another reason mobile marketing is so important is that people tend to be more engaged when consuming content on their phones. In fact, according to a study by Google, *"61% of users said they would rather watch a video on their phone than on any other device."* This means that if you want your content to be seen by the most people and be most effective, you need to create videos designed for mobile viewing.

Finally, it's important to note that mobile marketing is for more than just big businesses. Small businesses can benefit from mobile marketing just as much as large businesses can. This is because mobile devices allow businesses to target specific audiences based on demographics such as location and age. So no matter what size your business is, you can benefit from using mobile marketing techniques.

Marketers need to make sure that their content is mobile-friendly

The use of mobile devices for internet browsing is on the rise, as is the use of mobile devices for marketing. To capitalize on this trend, marketers need to make sure that their content is mobile-friendly. This means ensuring that their websites are easy to navigate on a phone or tablet and that their images and videos are easy to view and share.

Another critical consideration for marketers is the use of push notifications. Push notifications allow marketers to send messages directly to a user's phone. They can promote content and offers or keep users updated on the latest news.

Push notifications can be a powerful tool for marketers, but they must be used carefully. They can quickly become annoying if they are used too frequently or if the messages are not relevant to the user.

Marketers who want to take advantage of the growing use of mobile devices need to make sure that their content is mobile-friendly. This means ensuring that their websites are easy to navigate on a phone or tablet and that their images and videos are easy to view and share. They also need to use push notifications carefully so they don't become annoying.

CHAPTER FIVE

Marketing to Gen Z

Generation Z is the demographic group that follows the Millennial generation

As marketers, we must understand how to connect with the newest generation of consumers – Gen Z. Born between 1995 and 2010, this group is already making an impact on the economy. They are digital natives who have never known a world without the internet. Gen Z is also diverse and multicultural.

So how do we reach this tech-savvy, diverse group? Here are three tips for online marketing to Gen Z:

1. Use social media wisely. Gen Z is highly connected and uses social media extensively. They expect brands to be where they are, so it's important to have a solid social media presence. But don't just post content for the sake of posting – make sure it's relevant and engaging.

2. Think mobile first. Gen Z grew up with cell phones and tablets, so they are comfortable using technology for everything from shopping to banking. Make sure your website and apps are mobile-friendly, and take advantage of other mobile technologies like geolocation and augmented reality.

3. Try new things. Gen Z is always looking for new experiences, so innovating and experimenting with new marketing tactics is important. Use tools like live streaming and Snapchat filters to reach this tech-savvy audience.

They have grown up with technology

Gen Z has grown up with technology and is comfortable with online marketing. Here are three tips for marketing to this generation online:

1. Use social media platforms that Gen Z is comfortable with; Gen Z is mainly on Snapchat, Instagram, and YouTube; be sure to use these platforms to reach out to them.

2. Use creative content. Gen Z responds well to creative content, so be sure to use videos, infographics, and other types of content that will capture their attention.

3. Speak their language. Gen Z communicates differently than older generations, so be sure to use language they understand when marketing to them online.

Their attention span is shorter than that of previous generations

According to Vision Critical, *"On average, Gen Z will pay attention to content for a span of eight seconds -- four less than millennials."* Gen Z is the most technologically savvy generation to date. They are constantly connected to their devices and the internet. This makes them a very engaged group when it comes to online marketing. However, because their attention span is shorter than previous generations, marketers need to be more creative and concise when reaching out to them.

Some practical ways to market to Gen Z online include short videos, memes, and interactive content. Additionally, marketers should ensure they use platforms that this generation is most engaged with; for example, Snapchat, Instagram, and YouTube are all popular among Gen Zers.

It is also important to be aware of the issues that matter to this generation. For example, climate change and gun violence are important topics to Gen Z and should be considered when crafting marketing campaigns.

Finally, it is essential to continuously test and measure the effectiveness of online marketing campaigns targeting Gen Z. Data from 2022 shows that Gen Z will make up more than 40% of all consumers, so it's important to start gearing your marketing strategy toward them now. This will help ensure that campaigns resonate with this demographic and generate the desired results.

They are attracted to visual content, so marketers need to make sure that their content is visually appealing

They are digital natives who have never known a world without social media. As a result, they are attracted to visual content. Marketers need to make sure that their content is visually appealing if they want to reach this demographic.

One way to do this is by using videos. Gen Z loves watching videos, and it's one of the most effective ways to grab their attention. For example, studies show that 90% of Gen Zers watch videos weekly. You can create engaging videos that appeal to this demographic by using creative storytelling and incorporating stylish visuals.

Another way to make your content visually appealing is by using infographics. Infographics are a great way to share information in an easy-to-digest format. Gen Zers are drawn to infographics because they are visually stimulating and provide a lot of information in a short amount of time. For example, you can create your infographics or find free templates online.

Finally, you can also use images on your website and social media posts. Images are eye-catching and help you stand out in a crowded newsfeed. Make sure that the images you use are high-quality and relevant to your brand.

By following these tips, you can create visually appealing content that will resonate with Gen Zers and help you achieve your marketing goals.

CHAPTER SIX

Marketing automation

Marketing automation is the use of software to automate marketing tasks

Several advantages come with using marketing automation software. The most obvious benefit is that it can save business owners time and energy. Automated marketing tools can help you stay organized and efficient, which is crucial when trying to run a successful online business. Additionally, marketing automation can help you improve your results by automating many of the tasks involved in marketing your products or services. This includes email marketing, lead nurturing, and social media campaigns.

When choosing a marketing automation tool, there are several factors to consider:

1. Ensure that the software you choose has all the features you need to automate your marketing tasks.
2. Make sure that the software is easy to use to get the most out of it.
3. It's also important to find a tool that is affordable and fits within your budget.

Marketing automation can be a precious tool for business owners looking to make money online. For example, you can save time and energy by automating everyday marketing tasks while improving your results. When choosing a marketing automation tool, make sure to consider the features offered and be sure to select one that is easy to use.

It can help to save time and improve efficiency

Online marketing automation is a process of using software to complete repetitive tasks quickly and efficiently. This can include tasks such as sending out emails, managing social media campaigns, or analyzing data. Automation can help business owners save time and improve their efficiency when marketing their business.

Many different software programs can be used for marketing automation. Some of the more popular ones include HubSpot, Infusionsoft, and Marketo. These programs allow you to automate various tasks, including email marketing, web form submissions, and even lead scoring.

Automation can be an extremely valuable tool for business owners who are looking to make money online. It can help you save time and improve your efficiency, allowing you to focus on other aspects of your business.

However, it is important to use marketing automation wisely, as it can also have negative effects

Marketing automation tools allow you to automate your marketing tasks, saving time and energy. However, it is vital to use them wisely, as they can also have negative effects.

For example, if you are using an automated email system, be sure to test the system thoroughly before sending out any emails. Otherwise, you may send out messages that are not formatted correctly or contain errors. This can damage your reputation and make you look unprofessional.

In addition, it is important to be aware of the potential for spamming with marketing automation tools. If you are not careful, you may send out too many messages to your subscribers, which could lead to them unsubscribing from your list or marking your messages as spam.

Finally, it is important to remember that marketing automation should be used as something other than a substitute for personal interaction. Although automated tools can help you reach more people and generate more leads, they should be used to supplement human interaction. Instead, use them to increase your personal interactions and to help you reach a larger audience.

CHAPTER SEVEN

Trends in SEO

Search engine optimization is an integral part of online marketing

SEO is an ever-evolving field, and search engines are continually updating their algorithms to provide the best possible search results for their users. As a result, SEO techniques that worked a few years ago may no longer be effective today. Here are some of the most critical trends in SEO today:

1. Mobile optimization

With more and more people using their smartphones to search for information online, it is increasingly important for businesses to have mobile-friendly websites. In addition, search engine ranking algorithms now consider the mobile-friendliness of websites when ranking them in search results.

2. Content marketing

Content is now king in SEO, and businesses must focus on creating high-quality content to engage and educate their target audience. This content can then be used to attract links from other websites, which is still one of the most important factors when it comes to ranking in search results.

3. Social media marketing

Social media has become an important part of SEO, with many people discovering websites and products through social media channels like Facebook and Twitter. Businesses should ensure they are active on social media and use it to drive traffic to their website.

It can help to improve a website's visibility and organic search results

As technology evolves, so does SEO. While the basics of SEO remain the same, such as optimizing a website for specific keywords and using backlinks to improve authority, new trends in SEO are constantly emerging. Some of the latest trends include using artificial intelligence to improve website ranking, optimizing voice search, and using videos to improve engagement.

SEO is constantly evolving to keep up with technological advancements. One of the latest trends in SEO is using artificial intelligence (AI) to improve website ranking. This involves using AI-powered chatbots to answer customer questions and provide relevant information on the website. This can help improve the customer experience and ensure they find what they are looking for on the website.

Another trend in SEO that is growing in popularity is optimizing websites for voice search. With the rise of voice assistants such as Siri and Alexa, more people are using voice search to find information online. As a result, websites need to optimize their content for voice search to rank higher in search results.

The use of videos is another trend that is growing in popularity among SEO professionals. Videos can improve website engagement and help tell a story about a company or product. They can also be used to increase brand awareness and drive traffic to a website.

Some trends in SEO include:

1. Use keywords and related keywords in content to rank higher in search engine results pages (SERPs).

2. The use of structured data and schema markup to help Google better understand the content on a website.

3. The increasing importance of mobile SEO, as more and more people use smartphones and other mobile devices to access the internet.

4. One trend in SEO is using more long-tail keywords because they are more specific and targeted and, therefore, can result in higher conversion rates.

5. Another trend is using more video content, which is a highly effective way to engage your audience and boost your SEO rankings.

6. Finally, another trend is increasing social media platforms like Twitter and Facebook to promote your website and increase its visibility.

CHAPTER EIGHT

Content marketing in 2023

Content marketing is a type of marketing that focuses on creating and distributing valuable content

In 2023, content marketing will be more important than ever. With so much online competition, businesses must create valuable content that stands out from the rest to attract and retain customers. This means that businesses will need to invest in quality content creation and distribution strategies, and they will also need to find ways to make their content more engaging and interactive.

One trend likely to continue in 2023 is using videos and other multimedia content. Videos are a great way to engage customers and can effectively convey a message or tell a story.

In 2023, businesses will continue to use videos to connect with their customers and create a more personal connection.

Another trend likely to continue in 2023 is the use of social media for content distribution. Social media platforms are great for reaching a large audience quickly and easily. In 2023, businesses will still use social media to get their content in front of as many people as possible.

It can help to build relationships with potential and current customers

In 2023, content marketing will still be an effective way to build relationships with potential and current customers. While other forms of marketing may become more popular or commonplace, content marketing will continue to provide value for businesses looking to connect with their customers.

One of the main benefits of content marketing is that it helps businesses to create trust and credibility with their customers. By sharing valuable, relevant, and engaging content, businesses can show that they know what they're talking about and that they care about their customers. This can help create a stronger connection with customers and encourage them to return to your site or business.

Content marketing is also a great way to keep your brand top-of-mind with your target audience. When you consistently share exciting and relevant content, you increase the chances that people will think of your brand when they need your products or services. As competition in the marketplace continues to grow, it's more important than ever to stand out from the crowd. And content marketing can help you do just that.

Ultimately, content marketing is a great way to connect with your customers and help your business grow. By providing valuable information and connecting with your audience, you can build a foundation of trust that will lead to increased sales and success in the future.

Some trends in content marketing include:

1. The continued growth of content marketing, as businesses recognize its effectiveness in reaching customers.

2. The increasing use of video content, as it becomes more widely understood that people prefer watching videos to reading text.

3. The rise of artificial intelligence and machine learning will allow businesses to create more personalized content for their customers.

CHAPTER NINE

Predictions for the future of online marketing

The future of online marketing is ever-changing

As technologies advance, so does online marketing. Over the next decade, we can expect even more innovative and interactive ways for businesses to reach consumers online. Some of the most exciting possibilities include:

1. Virtual and augmented reality: As these technologies become more advanced and widespread, we can expect more businesses to use them to create immersive marketing experiences. For example, a furniture store could use virtual reality to allow customers to explore a virtual version of their

showroom, or a restaurant could use augmented reality to show diners how their food will look before they order.

2. Intelligent assistants: With the increasing popularity of intelligent assistants like Siri and Alexa, more businesses will likely use them to interact with customers. This could involve answering customer questions, processing orders, and providing product recommendations.

3. Increased use of chatbots: Chatbots are already starting to play a significant role in online marketing, and we can expect this trend to continue in the years ahead. They offer several advantages over traditional forms of communication, such as convenience and affordability. Additionally, chatbots are becoming increasingly sophisticated and can now handle a wide range of tasks.

Marketers need to be prepared for change

1. The internet is constantly evolving, and so is online marketing. As technology changes and new platforms emerge, marketers need to be prepared for change and be able to adapt quickly.

2. Online marketing will become even more dynamic and innovative in the future. We will see new platforms and technologies emerge, and marketers will need to be skilled in using them all.

3. To stay ahead of the competition, businesses must invest in online marketing strategies that keep up with the latest trends. This means allocating resources to digital marketing teams constantly researching new technologies and platforms.

Some predictions for the future of online marketing include:

1. More focus on mobile marketing- With most internet users now accessing the web via their phones, businesses will need to shift more of their focus towards mobile marketing to reach their target audience. This could include developing more targeted ads, optimizing websites for mobile browsers, and using location-based services to send alerts and special offers to customers near the business.

2. More video content- Video content is becoming increasingly popular online, as it is a great way to grab people's attention and engage them more effectively than just text or images alone. In the future, businesses will likely invest more in creating video content for their websites and social media pages to attract and keep customers engaged.

3. Greater use of artificial intelligence- As artificial intelligence technology continues to develop, businesses will start to use it for online marketing purposes. This could include chatbots that can help customers with product inquiries or suggestions or

recommendation algorithms that can recommend products or services based on a customer's past browsing history.

CHAPTER TEN

5 things you can do in 2023 to dominate online marketing

If you want to stay ahead of the curve in online marketing, you need to be willing to change with the times. What worked last year might not work this year, and what works today might not work tomorrow. That's why staying on top of the latest trends and developments in online marketing is so important. So here are five things you can do in 2023 to stay ahead of the competition.

1. **Make use of AI and machine learning.**
AI and machine learning are two of the most important emerging technologies that will shape the future of online

marketing. By harnessing the power of these technologies, you'll be able to create highly personalized and targeted marketing campaigns that will resonate with your audience on a deeper level. In 2023, using AI and machine learning should be a top priority for any online marketer who wants to stay ahead of the competition.

To use AI and machine learning in your marketing campaigns, you must first understand these technologies and how they can be used to improve your results. AI is a technology that enables machines to learn and evolve on their own, while machine learning is a method of teaching computers to learn by example. These technologies can be used in several ways to improve your marketing campaigns, including:

1. Automated segmentation and targeting: With the help of AI and machine learning, you can automatically segment your audience based on their interests and preferences. This will allow you to target them with highly personalized content relevant to them.

2. Predictive analytics: By using predictive analytics, you can use past data to predict your audience's behavior and identify trends that will help you create more effective campaigns.

3. Automated content creation: With the help of AI, you can create automated content tailored to your audience's needs.

This will help you save time and produce more engaging and relevant content.

2.   Use data-driven marketing strategies.

Data-driven marketing is more important than ever before. By 2023, it's estimated that data will account for 44% of all global business value. Businesses that don't leverage data-driven marketing strategies will be at a serious disadvantage compared to their competitors.

So what can you do to start using data in your marketing? Start by collecting data from your website visitors and customers. Use tools like Google Analytics to track website traffic and customer behavior. Use customer surveys to gather feedback about customer needs and preferences. And use social media listening tools to track conversations about your brand online.

Once you have the data, it's important to analyze it and extract insights. Use data analysis tools like Excel or Tableau to help you find trends and patterns in the data. Once you have the insights, it's time to create marketing campaigns tailored to your target audience. Use the data to understand what content they prefer, what kind of messaging resonates with them, and what kind of offers they're most likely to respond to.

Data-driven marketing is one of the most effective ways to reach your target audience and achieve your marketing goals. By using data-driven strategies, you'll be able to create laser-focused campaigns on your target market, resulting in higher conversion rates and ROI.

3.   Employ influencer marketing tactics.

In 2023, it's estimated that businesses will spend $10 billion on influencer marketing. However, this number will only continue to grow as social media platforms become more popular and businesses realize the power of influencers in promoting their products and services.

There are a few reasons why influencer marketing is so effective:
1.   People trust word-of-mouth recommendations more than any other type of advertising.
2.   People are likelier to act on recommendations from someone they know and trust than strangers.
3.   Social media platforms make it easy for businesses to connect with influencers and spread their message far and wide.

If you still need to use influencer marketing tactics, now is the time. It's a powerful way to reach a large audience without spending much money, and the results can be impressive. So don't wait - start building relationships with influencers in your industry today!

4.   **Create interactive content.**

Gone are the days when static content like blog posts and whitepapers cut it with today's audiences—they're craving something more engaging and interactive. In 2023, businesses need to create more interactive content like quizzes, infographics, polls, and surveys. Not only will this type of content capture your audience's attention, but it will also help you collect valuable data that you can use to improve your overall marketing strategy.

A stat from 2022 shows that businesses that use interactive content see a 66% increase in leads. This is because interactive content is more engaging and can help you collect valuable data from your audience.

For example, my company recently created a quiz about social media marketing. The quiz was very popular, and we gathered data about our audience's preferences and interests. We then used this data to create more relevant content and improve our overall marketing strategy.

Interactive content is the way to go if you want to create more engaging content. Not only will it help you capture your audience's attention, but it will also help you learn more about what they want and need.

5. **Take advantage of chatbots and messenger apps.**

Chatbots and messenger apps are becoming increasingly popular as platforms for businesses to interact with their customers on a more personal level. For example, in 2023, more businesses will use chatbots and messenger apps to provide customer support, answer questions, and promote their products or services. If you want to stay ahead of the competition, start experimenting with chatbots and messenger apps to hit the ground running when they become mainstream.

One reason why chatbots and messenger apps are so popular is that they offer an easy way for customers to get in touch with businesses. In 2023, there will be over 8 billion active Messenger users, meaning businesses that don't use Messenger will miss out on many potential customers.

Another reason chatbots and messenger apps are so popular is that they offer a more personalized experience for customers. By using chatbots and messenger apps, businesses can create a one-on-one interaction with their customers that isn't possible with other platforms. This allows businesses to build stronger relationships with their customers and create loyalty among them.

To stay ahead of the curve in online marketing, it is vital to be aware of the latest trends. This book provided a comprehensive look at the upcoming trends for 2023. It is a valuable resource for any marketer who wants to stay ahead of the competition.

Thank you for purchasing the book! As a marketing professional with years of experience in this field, this book contains valuable insights that can help you succeed in today's competitive business landscape.

Whether you are an experienced marketer or just starting, staying up-to-date with the latest trends and best practices in this dynamic field is important. Our book is a comprehensive guide that covers everything you need to know about marketing and advertising in 2023, including the latest strategies, tactics, and tools.

So if you are ready to take your marketing skills to the next level, please re-read our book and put the information it contains to good use.

Thanks again for your purchase, and I wish you all the best in your marketing endeavors.

Sincerely,

Brandon Raybon

References

HubSpot. (n.d.). *2022 marketing statistics, Trends & Data - the ultimate list of Digital Marketing stats*. HubSpot. Retrieved October 26, 2022, from https://www.hubspot.com/marketing-statistics

Marketing & Advertising curated news: WARC: The feed. WARC An Ascential Company. (n.d.). Retrieved October 11, 2022, from https://www.warc.com/content/feed/warc-adspend-outlook-2022-23-what-you-need-to-know/7142

The 2017 U.S. mobile app report. Comscore, Inc. (n.d.). Retrieved October 26, 2022, from https://www.comscore.com/Insights/Presentations-and-Whitepapers/2017/The-2017-US-Mobile-App-Report

The dominant global marketing trends of 2023: MarcomCentral. MarcomCentral | Digital Asset Management Solution | Manage Your Marketing Brand. (2022, September 19). Retrieved October 11, 2022, from https://marcom.com/2023-global-marketing-trends/d

Time Flies: U.S. adults now spend nearly half a day interacting with media. Nielsen. (2022, July 21). Retrieved October 26, 2022, from https://www.nielsen.com/insights/2018/time-flies-us-adults-now-spend-nearly-half-a-day-interacting-with-media/

Williams, R. (2019, August 14). *Gen Z seeks all-day entertainment from mobile devices, study says*. Marketing Dive. Retrieved October 26, 2022, from https://www.marketingdive.com/news/gen-z-seeks-all-day-entertainment-from-mobile-devices-study-says/560868/

Made in the USA
Monee, IL
07 April 2023